Under
Lecture

By:
Damien Jack, PEHP

Edited By:
L. Ken Collins, II

Under the Living Arch©
Charlotte, NC • 2016

@
Under the Living Arch – Lectures of the Chapter
Copyright© 2016 by Damien Jack
Published 2016
Printed in the United States of America

ISBN: 9781530753284

All rights reserved. No part of this publication may be reproduced, stored in a retrieval system, or transmitted in any form or by any means, electronic, mechanical, photocopying, recording, or otherwise, without the prior permission of the publisher.

Jack, Damien., 1979 –
Under the Living Arch – Lectures of the Chapter
/Prince Hall Royal Arch Esotericism/Prince Hall York Rite Lectures/ Prince Hall Freemasonry /

Acknowledgements

First I would like to give all glory and honor to the Great I Am, from whom all blessings flow. I would like to acknowledge my instructor in HRAM, PEHP Ivey Wilson and my "Father' in Masonry for guiding me through this journey.

To my editor, L. Ken Collins, I can never thank you enough for planting the seed in me to take this step of faith.

To my Companion, PEHP Michael Duncan, thank you not just for the cover design, but for being there whenever I needed your assistance. I would like to acknowledge my chapter, the BACK TO BACK Chapter of the Year in the jurisdiction of North Carolina Excelsior Chapter No. 44.

I must give a special thanks to my Most Excellent Grand High Priest William A. Cooke for having faith in me to allow me to serve as Excellent Grand Lecturer for the Most Excellent Grand Chapter of Holy Royal Arch Masons of North Carolina – PHA!

Thank you to PEHP Ronnie Durrett in Maryland for his support.

To my Classmates PEHPs Clarence Trayhnam and Eddie Tucker thank you for your instruction and guidance. To Companions Stanley Brooks and Francois Evans, thank you for always believing and supporting me.

To all of my Companions who have read, enjoyed and been inspired by what I have written, to my closest brothers who have encouraged me along the way, I say thank you.

Last, but certainly not least, I thank my Queen and my best friend Na'Shota Lytle. Your guidance, support and love are the things that keep me going. You believed in me at times more than I believed in myself. With you in my corner there's nothing I can't accomplish. I love you and thank you.

Introduction

The Capitular Rite of Freemasonry, better known as the "Red House" is made up of four degrees or ceremonies consisting of the Mark Master Degree, Past Master Degree, Most Excellent Master Degree and the Holy Royal Arch. The legends, allegory and symbolism of these degrees continue the story of Symbolic Masonry as it relates: to the history of King Solomon's Temple, after its completion and dedication; its destruction by the Chaldeans and the Babylonian captivity of the Jews along with the history con the erection of the Second Temple by Zerubbabel. This Rite of Masonry also provides a distinct connection with the Third Degree in the "recovery of certain secrets", which were presumed to be lost when Hiram Abiff was slain.

Within the teachings of this Rite, there is no more altruistic instruction or loftier sentiment expressed in any degree of Freemasonry than in the charge to the newly made Most Excellent Master and no brother of any degree within this body can be too often be reminded of its content: "It is one of you great duties , as a Most Excellent Master, to DISPENSE LIGHT AND TRUTH to the uniformed Mason; and I need not remind you of the impossibility of complying with this obligation without possessing an accurate acquaintance with the lectures of each degree. If you are not already completely conversant with the degrees heretofore conferred on you, remember that an indulgence, prompted by the belief that you would apply yourself with double diligence to become so, has induced the brethren to accept you. Let it therefore be your unremitting study to acquire such a degree of knowledge and information as shall enable you to discharge with propriety the various duties incumbent upon you.

It has been said; "there is no greater gift man can give his fellow man than knowledge" and the compilation of lectures within this book is but one Companion's labor of service to dispense light and truth to our lessor informed brethren and those seeking "further light in masonry".

Companion William A. Cooke, KYGCH
Most Excellent Grand High Priest
Most Excellent Grand Chapter Holy Royal Arch Mason Jurisdiction of NC

Table of Contents

The Character of a Royal Arch Mason	Page 10
Mark Well	Page 14
Peace & Harmony	Page 17
Rejected Stone	Page 21
Lost and Found	Page 25
I Am That I Am	Page 29
The Charge of a Holy Royal Arch Mason	Page 32
The Second Temple	Page 37
The Tabernacle	Page 42
The Temple and The Tabernacle	Page 49
Words of the Veils	Page 53
Your Latter is Greater	Page 57
Walking the Veils	Page 62

What Does it Mean to be Exalted	**Page 66**
When the Work is Complete	**Page 70**
Judah, Ephraim, Rueben and Dan	**Page 73**
About the Author	**Page 79**

Chapter 1

The Character of a Royal Arch Mason

"When engaged in the pursuit of Truth, the great object of Masonic study, we should have the courage of the Lion; the intelligence of Man; the patience of the Ox; and the swiftness of the Eagle."

Ever since coming into Masonry, we have learned that Truth is a divine attribute and the foundation of every virtue. As we learn in our further travels in Masonry, we are in pursuit of Truth to the point we ask just as Pontius Pilate asked Jesus in John 18:38, "What is Truth?" In understanding this, we must know that the pursuit is difficult and requires those characteristics displayed in the Lion, the Man, the Ox and the Eagle.

We have seen these Four Living Creatures throughout our history, and throughout the Bible. It has been said in Matthew Henry's Concise Commentary that these creatures represented the 4 Living Gospels; Matthew, Mark, Luke and John. In the Book of Ezekiel, there are the Cherubim whose role is to guard God's Holy domain and presence from any sin and corruption. They are sometime known as the throne angels as they are seen to be around the throne of God.

Webster's Dictionary defines Courage as: "mental or moral strength to venture, persevere, and withstand danger, fear, or difficulty." What can be more courageous than a lion? The lion has been symbolized throughout the Bible as being fearless and majestic. It is said in Proverbs 30:30 that: *"A lion is strongest among beasts, and turneth not away for any."* This shows that in the face of danger, whether pursuing or being pursued, the lion is always steadfast. Christ himself, who's symbolized by the lion, never wavered from the duty he was assigned. No matter the obstacles he faced, he kept pressing forward. In becoming Master Masons we learned our paths would be beset with dangers and difficulties, even our lives themselves may be threatened. But we must remember John 16:33 which states: *"I have said these things to you, that in me you may have peace. In the world you will have tribulation. But take heart; I have overcome the world,"* as well as 2 Timothy 1:7 which states: *"For God did not give us spirit of fear, but of power, of love and of a sound mind."*

Intelligence is defined by Webster's Dictionary as: "the ability to learn or understand things or to deal with new or difficult situations" Intelligence is held in higher regard than physicality as Proverbs 24:5 states, *"The wise are mightier than the strong, and those with knowledge grow stronger and stronger."* A word synonymous with Intelligence is Reason. This is what sets Man apart from any of God's creations. Although Man was God's last creation we learn that Man is the "glorious climax of all created things."

Man is set apart from God's other creations because of the way Man was created and what he was given. Genesis 1:26 states, *"And God said, Let us make man in our image, after our likeness: and let them have dominion over the fish of the sea, and over the fowl of the air, and over the cattle, and over all the earth, and over every creeping thing that creepeth upon the earth."* Being made in His image Man was given the ability to reason, communicate, and make moral decisions. This is a reminder of the Fourth Noble Science – Logic, which teaches us how to develop clear and distinct ideas and prevents you from being misled by similitudes and resemblances.

The next characteristic, Patience, is defined by Webster's Dictionary as: "able to remain calm and not become annoyed when waiting for a long time or when dealing with problems or difficult people." Patience is defined in Galatians 5:22-23 as one of the fruits of the Holy Spirit. Whether it's called longsuffering, endurance, or waiting, we learn that patience produces character as Romans 5:4 exclaims and through patience God's timing, power and love is revealed. The ox has been a symbol of patience and determination. The ox is mainly used for heavy labor such as plowing. Their patience allows them to labor for long period of time obeying the command to press forward over and over again. This relates to us because we must be patient in our pursuit and know that in His time we may see the fruits of our labor.

The final characteristic is Swiftness. To be swift, according to Webster's Dictionary is to be "quick to respond." The swiftness of an eagle takes on many forms. Job saw the swiftness of an eagle as a symbol of the brevity of life. Jonathan and Saul's lives were described as being swifter than eagles. In the book of Jeremiah, the swiftness of the eagle described God's judgment. Even King Solomon himself was amazed by the way of the eagle in the air. The eagle was the most mentioned bird throughout the Bible. This majestic bird is admired for its wings, the way it soars through the sky and its incredible vision. Just as the eagle is swift to catch its prey, we must be just as swift spreading the truth we've pursued to those who are willing to receive it.

In conclusion, it takes courage to pursue truth, to stand firm and persevere even in the face of adversity. It takes intelligence to pursue truth, to truly understand what's right and grow stronger in the knowledge obtained. It takes patience to pursue truth, to know that things will take time and even when you don't think you reached your goal, keep pressing on. Finally, it takes swiftness to pursue truth, to be quick to stop those who spread falsehoods and help those ready to receive truth. These internal characteristics are what make us better men. Continue to study, continue to grow and continue to improve.

-Holiness to the Lord –

Chapter 2

Mark Well!

"And the LORD said unto me, Son of man, mark well, and behold with thine eyes, and hear with thine ears all that I say unto thee concerning all the ordinances of the house of the LORD, and all the laws thereof; and mark well the entering in of the house, with every going forth of the sanctuary."

– Ezekiel 44:5

This passage of scripture is alluded from the real word given as Mark Master Mason. As we have learned In Masonry, the password and real word is given to each degree for a particular reason. Let's discover the reasoning for the use of this word.

The scripture that this word is taken from is found in Ezekiel Chapter 44. Ezekiel was a priest who, according to Ezekiel 1:1 received a vision from the Lord when he was 30 years old. During this time the people of Israel were in exile due to their continuous rebellion against God. Because of this the majority of Ezekiel's prophecy spoke of judgment and the remission of sins. God also showed Ezekiel the reconstruction of the Temple and the entering of the Glory of God.

In Ezekiel 44, God took Ezekiel to the Temple for the third time. He took Ezekiel to the East, where he noticed all the gates except this particular gate was shut. It's stated in Ezekiel 44:2-3, *"Then said the LORD unto me; This gate shall be shut, it shall not be opened, and no man shall enter in by it; because the LORD, the God of Israel, hath entered in by it, therefore it shall be shut. It is for the prince; the prince, he shall sit in it to eat bread before the LORD; he shall enter by the way of the porch of that gate, and shall go out by the way of the same."*

Afterwards Ezekiel was taken to the north gate where he witnessed the Glory of the Lord filling the Temple. According to Ezekiel 44:4; he looked upon his face and the Lord said unto Ezekiel, what was quoted in the aforementioned scripture. The Lord then gave Ezekiel instructions on what to say to his people of Israel. The Lord told Ezekiel to remind his people why they were placed in exile, and the disappointment of the Levites. But he also spoke of the resurrection of His people, and according to Ezekiel 44:15-31, the Levites were given strict instructions on how to act, minister, and judge within the Temple.

So how does this passage of scripture apply to us? To mark, according to Webster's Dictionary means, "to take notice of or observe." Ezekiel was told by the Lord to observe well by hearing and seeing everything that would take place from entering the sanctuary and thereafter. Upon your entrance into Holy Royal Arch Masonry, you were given this word to pay close attention to everything that would take place thereafter. You would Mark Well how the rejected stone soon became the cornerstone. You would

Mark Well the completion and dedication of the Temple. You would Mark Well its destruction, the captivity and release of a people. You would Mark Well the rebuilding of God's house.

As Holy Royal Arch Masons we should Mark Well the lessons we have been taught. We should Mark Well the working tools we have been given to improve ourselves. We should Mark Well the characteristics and means by which we should carry ourselves. Most of all, we should Mark Well how to worship that name which was once lost. In all that you do through life, take heed to those two (2) words: Mark Well!

-Holiness to the Lord-

Chapter 3

Peace & Harmony

"Wherefore laying aside all malice, and all guile, and hypocrisies, and envies, and all evil speakings."

– 1 Peter 2:1

This particular passage of scripture starts the charge for the opening of the Mark Master Mason degree. It may seem basic, but that one opening sentence describes what we strive for not just in Masonry but all of humanity, Peace & Harmony. It said that peace and harmony should be enjoyed at our meetings, as Scottish Rite Masons we fight to produce peace and harmony. What makes peace and harmony so important?

Since our first meeting as Master Masons, we've been told by the Sr. Warden that harmony is the support of all institutions, especially this of ours. It is his duty to ensure that none may go away dissatisfied, but it's not until the degree of Mark Master Mason that we notice dissatisfaction and disharmony. But before continuing this path, let's first understand what peace and harmony is.

Webster's Dictionary describes peace as, "freedom from oppressive thoughts or emotions." Harmony is defined as, "internal calm; an agreement or concord." In the parable found in Matthew

20:1-16, we find that some of the workers are in disharmony because they worked longer than some and felt they deserved to receive more wages than others. Far too often we see this Masonry, where Brothers or Companions are in discord because they feel that they deserve something over someone else. Some believe that brothers should not be in the position they're in, or receive the accolades they do, or even move forward with their journey just because the person in discord has been in the organization longer than the other. Due to this disharmony, you have exactly what 1 Peter 2:1 talks about; malice, doing things against that brother; hypocrisy, acting in a way that they know they wouldn't want to be treated, envy and evil speakings, talking behind the brothers back.

We not only see this in Masonry, we see this in life. We've all experienced the envy of others who watched us succeed in multiple aspects of our lives and witnessed the accolades we received. We hear of those speaking evil against us because they feel they deserve what we received and more, maybe because they have been doing those things longer or because they feel their work incomparable to others. Whatever the reason, peace and harmony cannot exist.

What we first must understand is that we cannot have peace without harmony. As stated before harmony is an internal calm and an agreement. First let's look at the agreement. In the parable, the overseer promised every worker he hired a penny for their work, not how long they worked. This parable was to show that it's not the length of the time that you put in the vineyard that God is worried about, but the quality of work. And whether you gave your life to Him decades ago or right on your deathbed, he still promised you a place in his many mansions. The same can be said for Masonry. It doesn't matter how long you've been a Mason, what matters is the work you put into it. The promise is still the same, to make better men using learning, subduing their passions and improving themselves. The reward, Last Sad Rites.

Secondly, you must have harmony within yourself. As an Entered Apprentice, you were given the common gavel to chip away at the rough ashlar, but some things require just a bit more force hence the reason for the Chisel and Mallet. When properly used as taught, we can curb ambition, depress envy and moderate. It is here we find our internal calm, it is here we can produce peace or freedom from oppressive thoughts or emotions.

Peace and Harmony come when you realize that as Masons our journeys are different, but we are aiming for the same goal and destination. Peace and Harmony come when you don't compare your journey with others when you realize that your rewards will come in due time, most importantly when you're able to work to achieve something bigger than yourself. It is then harmony and peace can be enjoyed at our meeting which no other society can afford.

"Now may the Lord of peace himself give you his peace at all times and in every situation. The Lord be with you all."
– 2 Thessalonians 3:16

-Holiness to the Lord-

Chapter 4

Rejected Stone

As we look back at the Mark Master Mason degree, we know that this degree is dedicated to the keystone, which is later known as the capstone. The capstone marked the completion of King Solomon's Temple, but for a small period this capstone was nowhere to be found. This of course was due to the Overseers not recognizing it for what it was heaving it over into a pile of rubbish. We later learn the rejected stone became the cornerstone of the Temple.

Let us stop and look for a brief minute at two (2) reasons why the stone which our GMHA created was rejected. First, it was not like the other pieces of work that were brought up for inspection. The Overseers had strict instruction to only accept those that were good, true and square. One may say that because the stone did not fit a certain description it was rejected. Secondly, no one knew what to make of it. The Senior and Junior Overseers suffered the stone to pass because of its singular beauty, but the Master Overseer saw fit to have it thrown away. It would suggest that because they have become accustomed to things being one way, they could not handle something different. In the end King Solomon reprimanded the Overseers and mentioned three (3) times about the passage of scripture which states: *"The stone that the builders rejected now has become the cornerstone,"* Psalm 118:22

We learn that Jesus Himself was the stone the builders rejected. Before His coming the people were used to following Moses' Law, but here comes Jesus, in Matthew 16:18 we learn: *"I also say to you that you are Peter, and upon this rock I will build My church; and the gates of Hades will not overpower it."* Jesus was building the church of Salvation and those who believed in Him would have everlasting life.

Of course He was rejected by men, because first, He was not like any other priest or prophet the people of Israel were used to and second, no one knew what to make of Him. Now He is the foundation for his building. He said in Matthew 16:19: "I will give you the keys of the kingdom of heaven; and whatever you bind on earth shall have been bound in heaven, and whatever you loose on earth shall have been loosed in heaven."

How is the keystone related to Jesus? As previously explained the keystone was first rejected by the Overseers and later became the completion of the temple. The keystone placed between the two pillars representing the terrestrial and celestial bodies. Symbolically, the keystone represents the transition from the terrestrial to the celestial as we learn in John 14:6, *"Jesus answered, I am the way, the truth and the life. No one comes to the father except through me."*

Jesus was not the only one in the Bible who was rejected. Look at Joseph, the youngest of Jacob's 11 children. Joseph was favored by his father and that made his brothers jealous. He was rejected by being sold into slavery, but as the story is told he becomes the cornerstone during the time of famine.

So how does this relate to us, not just as Royal Arch Masons, but as Men? 1 Peter 2:4-7 tells us: *"And coming to Him as to a living stone which has been rejected by men, but is choice and precious in the sight of God, you also, as living stones, are being built up as a spiritual house for a holy priesthood, to offer up spiritual sacrifices acceptable to God through Jesus Christ."* For this is contained in scripture: *"Behold, I lay in Zion a choice stone, a precious corner stone, and he who believes in him will not be disappointed."* Now to you who believe, this stone is precious. But to those who do not believe, *"The stone the builders rejected has become the cornerstone."*

This scripture reminds us we also are living stones. As Freemasons we are builders, and it is our job to use the tools we were given to prepare ourselves for that spiritual building. As Entered Apprentice we laid our cornerstone when we were placed in the Northeast corner. We were taught that the start of any building begins in the Northeast corner, there which to lay our foundation. Have you made that precious stone your foundation?

We are living stones, therefore there's something unique about each and every one of us and just like that precious stone we have been rejected in some form or fashion; possibly because we didn't fit into the mold of the crowd, or our beliefs were unlike others, or maybe because we stood for what's right rather than rest on tradition.

Whatever the reason may be we all have faced rejection. But look where you are now. It reminds me of a secular song that said, "Back then they didn't want me.." I won't finish the rest. Because you stand on that precious stone you have become the cornerstone in some aspect of your life. Webster defines cornerstone as: *"an important quality or feature on which a particular thing depends or is based."* You are now the cornerstone of your family, your job, your lodge, etc.

What's beautiful about you as a living stone is that although you are different, just like the Junior and Senior Overseers, there are those who see the beauty in you. There were those who saw the beauty in Jesus, they became his disciples, his congregation to spread his message. He faced many like the Master Overseer who did not know what to do with Him and heaved him over, but now... So when you face those like the Master Overseer always remember this, "Sometimes rejection is God's protection and a set up for your projection."

-Holiness to the Lord-

Chapter 5

Lost & Found

"I once was lost, but now I'm found, was blind but now I see."
— John Newton

The transition from Symbolic Masonry to Capitular Masonry is one of tragedy. GMHA is gone, the Temple is incomplete and the Master's word is lost. Many brothers are enticed with finding the "lost" word as a major reason for coming into this Order. What about the symbolism of losing and finding what you've lost?

First, I must remind you that we have learned as Fellow Crafts that Masonry is interwoven, or blended together. So sometimes we have to move between different degrees in order to understand what's happening where we are. With that being said, I believe it's important to give a brief explanation on how we have arrived at the point of the word being "lost." Scottish Rite Masons are aware that the word was discovered in preparation of building King Solomon's Temple. This word is considered by Scottish Rite Masons to be Ineffable, or too powerful to be described or expressed as Webster's Dictionary defines it. The mere mention of this causes flashes of lightning, rumbling of thunder and trembling of the earth, hence the reason the word is communication in a particular fashion within the Order.

Upon discovering the word, it was decided that this word would only be given at the completion of the Temple to those who were found worthy and could only be communicated when three are present. I will note that Scottish Rite Masons are also aware that the word discovered in a similar manner to how it was found, but I will discuss that in more detail later.

Now to the point where the word was lost. Lost, according to Webster's Dictionary, is defined as "something that has been taken away." In this case the ability to receive the word was taken away because of three ruffians who decided they wanted the word at that point in time. The ruffians were told that in due time and if found worthy they would receive the word, but that was not good enough for them and because of their actions the word was lost.

Proverbs 20:21 states, "*An inheritance obtained too early in life is not a blessing in the end.*" We learned that as EAs we travel ever East until we receive the divine password that admits us into his presence. This means we must work in the quarries and when the time comes we must show a suitable piece of our work. Symbolically this story is about us, in the midst of building our spiritual temple we become impatient and demand for something we're not yet ready to have. As result of our premature actions, we lose what we were not yet meant to have and the progress of building our temple is impeded.

Moving forward as Holy Royal Arch Masons we find the temple is destroyed and in preparation of rebuilding the temple we dig into the ruins to find any treasures that may be valuable. It is in the ruins that we find what was lost.

How does this relate to our lives? Many of us have not only impeded our progress, we have been like Zedekiah where we have ignored God's warning to the point that what we have built is destroyed. We find ourselves at a low point, but we also remember that He would not leave or forsake you as stated in Deuteronomy 31:6. In order to find what was lost we had to dig into the ruins of ourselves to find the word that has always been within us.

As stated earlier, the word was discovered in the similar way it was found. To discover the word it took three (3) people, to find the word it took three (3) trips. This too is symbolic because many times we are not ready to face our own truth and to truly discover and find the light we must uncover some things we don't want others to see. As Psalm 25:17 states, "Relieve the troubles of my heart, and free me from my anguish."

Companions, this particular lecture speaks of readiness, or Webster's Dictionary defines it, "being properly prepared." In our lives we have lost things or even people we were not yet ready to have. Many times we say to ourselves, "If I knew then what I know now," but in all honesty in the time, of "then" we were not yet ready and because of it we lost it. The prodigal son believed he was ready for his inheritance, and we all know the result of that story. What's beautiful about that story, however, is in the end no matter what we lose or how far we have become lost, once we have been found and brought to light, our Father will gladly welcome us home.

-Holiness to the Lord-

Chapter 6

I Am That I Am

"And Moses said unto God, Behold, when I come unto the children of Israel, and shall say unto them, The God of your fathers hath sent me unto you; and they shall say to me, What is his name? what shall I say unto them? And God said unto Moses, I AM THAT I AM: and he said, Thus shalt thou say unto the children of Israel, I AM hath sent me unto you. And God said moreover unto Moses, Thus shalt thou say unto the children of Israel, The LORD God of your fathers, the God of Abraham, the God of Isaac, and the God of Jacob, hath sent me unto you: this is my name for ever, and this is my memorial unto all generations."

-Exodus 3:13-15

Ever since coming into HRAM, I've always taken great pleasure in serving as the Principal Sojourner during an Exaltation, and reciting that passage of scripture has always been my favorite part. When we pray in this house we refer to the Lord as The Great I AM. When God told Moses His name, I have always wondered why he used this particular name. Allow me to share.

As we all know, God has many names. Within the Bible you will notice that "I Am" is found multiple times, mainly in the Book of John. Jesus who reminded the people in John 10:30 spoke these words, *"I and the Father are one."* In John 6:35 the Lord said, *"I AM the bread of life; he who comes to ME shall not hunger."* In John 8:12, he said, *"I

AM the light of the world, he who fallows ME shall not walk in darkness, but shall have the light of life." In John 10:9, the Lord said, "I AM the gate, if anyone enters through ME , he shall be saved, and shall go in an out and find pasture." John 10:11 states, "I AM the good shepherd, the good shepherd lays down his life for his sheep."

The Lord said in John 11:25, "I AM the resurrection and the life, he who believes in ME shall live even if he dies." He says in John 14:6, "I AM the way, the truth and the life; no one comes to the Father, but through ME." In John 15:1 the Lord says, "I AM the true vine and my Father is the vinedresser." Finally, in John 8:58, he says, "Truly, truly I say to you, before Abraham was born, I AM."

When you look at what has been listed, you come to the realization that only one name can describe God, and that is… I AM! God is whatever you need HIM to be in your situation. He cannot be defined as just one thing, because HE is so many things, hence the name I AM!

My Pastor wrote a song recently and the first five words of the song says, "You Don't Know My Story." Every Companion has a story, and God has been there each step of the way. Think back over your life, you don't have to go too far. When you were lacking, whether with food, finances or shelter, He was your Jehovah-Jireh, for He provided for you. When you were sick or hurting physically or emotionally, He was your Jehovah-Rapha, for He healed you. In the midst of your storm, He was Jehovah-Shammah, for He was there for you, He was Jehovah-Rohi, for He was your Shepherd who protected you, and He was Jehovah-Shalom, for He gave you peace. Moreover, when your storm was over when your enemies were defeated, you praised Jehovah-Nissi, for He gave you victory.

"I Am That I Am" a name that will be remembered for generations. It is the name of our creator. The name that assures us that through this life whatever goes on, you can call on The Great I Am, because HE IS whatever you need Him to be in your situation.

Let me also ask you this: Who are you in your situation? Whenever someone asks you, "How are you doing," your response always begins with "I Am." What comes behind that is very important. Proverbs 18:21 states: *"Death and life are in the power of the tongue: and they that love it shall eat the fruit thereof."* The words you speak are very powerful, not just in the lives of others, but to yourself. Matthew 12:37 states, *"For by your words you will be acquitted, and by your words you will be condemned."* The point is, the words you speak after "I Am" are a testament of what you believe. If you say "I Am sick," "I Am broke," then that is what you believe. But you have the power as stated in Luke 10:19, *"Behold, I give unto you power to tread on serpents and scorpions, and over all the power of the enemy: and nothing shall by any means hurt you."* Therefore, the next time you are asked how you are doing; speak positivity over your life.

-Holiness to the Lord-

Chapter 7

The Charge of a Holy Royal Arch Mason

Within the circle of Ancient Craft Masonry, much attention is given to the ritual, symbols and working tools. Each aspect together teaches lessons on how to improve yourself and become better men. There is, however, one aspect of Masonry that is oftentimes overlooked, the charge.

Charge, within the context of Masonry, has two (2) definitions according to Webster's Dictionary. The first definition is "to impose a task or responsibility on." The second definition is "to command or instruct." In essence you are instructed on how to conduct yourself according to the level you have reached.

Within the degrees of Holy Royal Arch Masonry, there are two (2) types of charges we receive; charges as candidates and as members. As a candidate of a Mark Master Mason, we learn that our duties become broader and as they do we should understand that our diligence should equal the amount of our duties. This leads us to our first charge, as we are compared to the stone the builders rejected. We are compared to the stone in two (2) ways both concerning conduct. First, we are taught that our conduct here in this life as we work in the quarries be good, square and true, so that when we're examined by God's square we won't be seen as unfit for the spiritual building

Second, the conduct which we display may cause to be rejected by those we called friends. It may cause envy, jealousy and persecution from those we once held dear to us. This is because just like the overseers who could not identify the mark or make of the stone, others will not be able to identify with the qualities you now possess. Just remember, you may be rejected by some, in the end you become the cornerstone.

Every degree we have received required us to be bound by an obligation. As Virtual Past Masters we learn that there have been those who were quick to come before the altar, take the obligations, then act as if it never happened. We are instructed to know that these obligations have been taken of our own free will and we should never lose sight of them. This is because the conduct we find in our obligations teaches us how to carry ourselves, so that when the outside world sees us in the character of Masons and Holy Royal Arch Masons, they will see in us we stand for what's right, we help those in need and we are guided by our kindness. Should we ever lose sight of the broadness of our obligations, we should keep close to us that rule and guide for our practice through life, that Great Masonic Light the Holy Bible.

Most Excellent Master, a congratulatory title received based on your Masonic abilities. It is here that you are charged to provide knowledge to uniformed brethren, and in doing so you MUST be well versed in the lectures and understanding of these degrees. This requires that you be diligent and study, as 2 Timothy 2:15 states,

"Study to show thyself approved unto God, a workman that needeth not to be ashamed, rightly dividing the word of truth."

Finally you've reached the sublime and august degree of Holy Royal Arch Mason. In this charge we are taught the importance of not recommending anyone into this Order who we feel does not have a firm grasp of the information in the prior degrees or who would not fulfill the obligations of the Order.

"With great power comes great responsibility." This was a quote used in a movie, but when you look at the charges received by candidates as he progresses in this Order, it becomes a great way to understand why you are given the duties you're given. The honor we confer and the merit we repose are the reasons why your duties become more extensive as you travel. Let us remember that we not only receive charges as candidates, we receive them as members.

As Mark Master Masons we're charged with the Scriptures of 1 Peter 2:15, 15-17 and Isaiah 28:16. These Scriptures teaches us that in order to grow in God's salvation, we must rid ourselves from all types of evil and constantly crave His word. Just a as God is considered the chief stone, the cornerstone of our lives, we, ourselves are considered living stones being prepared for that spiritual building. And as we respect God, love our brothers and continue to do well, our haters and enemies have no choice but to be silent.

Psalm 24 is the charge given to Most Excellent Masters. It is said that this particular Psalm was penned by David after retrieving the Ark of the Covenant and brought it back to Jerusalem. It was believed that when the Ark of Covenant came to Jerusalem God came with it. This passage of Scripture is seen as a prophecy for what takes place in this degree, which is the placing of the Ark into the Temple. We are instructed to be cleansed of our sins and God sees the purity of your heart. Only then can receive the blessings and righteousness of God.

Finally, as Holy Royal Arch Masons we are given instructions through 2 Thessalonians 3:6-16, which I consider to be one of the most important charges of all. Here we are taught the importance of work. These passages of scripture teach us the value of earning what you have. The work that we are set out to do is important for two (2) reasons; first, as 2 Thessalonians 3:10 says, *"For even when we were with you, we gave you this rule: "The one who is unwilling to work shall not eat."* It is self-explanatory that you must earn your keep. But let's not take "eating" in just a literal sense. How do you expect to enjoy the rewards of Masonry if you put nothing in it? This leads to the second reason, which is knowing that people are always watching what you do. Many years ago Charles Barkley did a commercial that stated, "I am not a role model." We as Sons of Light do not fall into that category. Others will imitate everything we do or do not do, so we must show them why people like Grand Worthy Matron Simmons uses the motto, "Hard Work Pays Off."

This charge also teaches to distance ourselves from those who choose not to work and disrupt the work that you do. Scripture calls them busybodies, or as Webster's Dictionary defines as a "meddling or prying person." We have all dealt with busybodies in our lives but as the charge teaches us, it should never stop us from doing good and being an example for others.

Companions, you have been charged. You have been given an enormous amount of responsibility. If you could not handle it, you would not be here. Remember the lessons you have been taught, not just for yourself but also for those coming after you as well as those who have lost their way.

-Holiness to the Lord-

Chapter 8

The Second Temple

There's much to be said of the Second Temple, first named to Zerubbabel and later to Herod the King. Approximately 538 BC, Cyrus began his reign in Persia as King. It was then the spirit of the Lord filled the spirit of Cyrus, who then proclaimed to rebuild the house of the Lord. In order to accomplish this task he released the Jewish people who had been in Babylonian Captivity for 70 years. Among those released from captivity was Zerubbabel, governor of the Persian province of Judah.

The temple was to be built near the ruins of King Solomon's Temple. The first item constructed was an alter to worship God as explained in Ezra 3:1-3: *"And when the seventh month was come, and the children of Israel were in the cities, the people gathered themselves together as one man to Jerusalem. Then stood up Jeshua [1] the son of Jozadak, and his brethren the priests, and Zerubbabel the son of Shealtiel, and his brethren, and builded the altar of the God of Israel, to offer burnt offerings thereon, as it is written in the law of Moses the man of God. And they set the altar upon his bases; for fear was upon them because of the people of those countries: and they offered burnt offerings thereon unto the Lord, even burnt offerings morning and evening."*

After building the altar, the foundation of the Temple was laid and the building of the second Temple commenced. According to Ezra 4, the building of the Temple was hindered due to opposition from the adversaries. Work on the Temple ceased for 15 years, and it was not until the reign Darius and the Immemorial Conversation (you have to travel further for more details) that the building continued. The second Temple was completed around 516 BC.

Upon its completion, the people were not pleased with this Temple. They compared to this Temple with King Solomon's Temple and those who had seen King Solomon's Temple in its glory was displeased as explained in Ezra 3:12: "But many of the older priests and Levites and family heads, who had seen the former temple, wept aloud when they saw the foundation of this temple being laid, while many others shouted for joy." But the Lord spoke through the prophet Haggai concerning the difference between the two (2) temples. Haggai 2:1-9 states: "on the twenty-first day of the seventh month, the word of the Lord came through the prophet Haggai: "Speak to Zerubbabel son of Shealtiel, governor of Judah, to Joshua son of Jozadak, the high priest, and to the remnant of the people. Ask them, 'Who of you is left who saw this house in its former glory? How does it look to you now? Does it not seem to you like nothing? But now be strong, Zerubbabel,' declares the Lord. 'Be strong, Joshua son of Jozadak, the high priest. Be strong, all you people of the land,' declares the Lord, 'and work. For I am with you,' declares the Lord Almighty. 'This is what I covenanted with you when you came out of Egypt. And my Spirit remains among you. Do not fear. "This is what the Lord Almighty says: 'In a little while I will once more shake the heavens and the earth, the sea and the dry land. I will shake all nations, and what is desired by all nations will come, and I will fill this house with glory,' says the Lord Almighty. 'The silver is mine and the gold is mine,' declares the Lord Almighty. 'The glory of this present house will be greater than the glory of the former house,' says the Lord Almighty. 'And in this place I will grant peace,' declares the Lord Almighty."

The glory of the second temple was indeed greater than the glory of the first temple for two (2) reasons. First, beginning in 19 BC, King Herod I began reconstructing the temple making it greater than the first temple. There were eight (8) gates that lead to the temple. A wall, which was named "The Wailing Wall," surrounded the area of the Holy Place, the Court of Gentiles, the Court of Women, and the Court for the Israelites.

The second, and most important, reason why the glory of this house was greater than the former is because on separate occasions Jesus himself visited the Temple. According to Luke 2:41-52, his people visited Jerusalem every year for Passover. When Joseph and his mother left, Jesus was not with them. They thought he was amongst the children of the other families so they continued on the journey. It was not until they returned home, they realized Jesus was not in the crowd. It took 3 days to find Jesus, and when they did, they found in the middle of the teachers of the temple asking and answering questions. His mother questioned why he had done this to them scaring them the way they did. Jesus responded in Luke 2:49, *"Why were you looking for me? Did you not know that I would be in the house of my father?"*

As an adult Jesus visited the Temple multiple times during Passover. When he first went to the Temple, according to John 2:16-19, he noticed that instead of worship, people were selling oxen, sheep and pigeons and there were also money changers. Jesus drove them of the Temple stating in John 2:16, *"Take these things away; do not make my Father's house a house of trade."*

When asked by the Jews what authority he had to do these things, his response was, *"Destroy this temple and in 3 days I will raise it up."* John 2:19. Afterwards, according to Matthew 21:14-17, the blind and the sick came into the Temple and Jesus began healing them and performing works of miracles. You could hear the children crying out *"Hosana, Son of David."*

Again during Passover Jesus was in the Temple teaching, and the chief priests and elders, according to Matthew 21:23-27 asked Jesus by what authority did he have to do the things he did. Jesus in turned asked one question: Did the baptism of John come from Man or from Heaven? Confused on how they should answer, the chief priests and elders responded that they did not know. In return Jesus responded, *"Neither will I tell you by what authority I do these things."* Matthew 21:27.

In Conclusion, we see that in the first Temple we witness the glory of God as He himself entered the Temple after dedication. In the second Temple, we witness the glory of the Son of Man, who died that we may have access to the Tree of Life. But there is still one temple left that needs to be explored. Do you know what the third temple is?

-Holiness to the Lord-

Chapter 9

The Tabernacle

At the opening of every Royal Arch Chapter, we are reminded that we are in a place representing the Tabernacle. The furnishings, colors, and tribes are all associated with the Tabernacle. What makes the Tabernacle so significant is that before the building of King Solomon's Temple and during the building of the second Temple, the Tabernacle was in place.

When Moses led the children of Israel out of Egypt, he was commanded by God to the top of Mt. Sinai. It was there Moses was commanded to build a tabernacle so the Lord may dwell among them as explained in Exodus 25:8-9, *"And let them make me a sanctuary; that I may dwell among them. According to all that I shew thee, after the pattern of the tabernacle, and the pattern of all the instruments thereof, even so shall ye make it."* God gives Moses specific instructions within the book of Exodus from Chapter 25 – Chapter 30 on how to build the Tabernacle and the furniture therein.

The sanctuary was divided into three (3) parts; the outer court, the brazen altar of sacrifice and, the Tabernacle itself. According to Exodus 27:9-19, the outer court was 100 cubits, or 150 feet, long and 50 cubits, or 75 feet wide. It was surrounded by a white linen fence, which was 5 cubits, or 7 ½ feet, high. On both the north and south side, the fence hung upon 20 pillars, and on the east and west side, the fence hung upon 10 pillars. Each pillar was set into a socket with a bronze base, and between them was a rod, which had which silver hooks upon them in order to hang the white linen. There was only one entrance into the sanctuary and that was on the East side, which was guarded by the tribe of Judah. The entrance was identified by its gate, which was 20 cubits, or 30 feet, long and was made by blue, scarlet and purple thread.

Within the outer court of the Tabernacle was the Brazen Altar and Brazen Laver. Exodus 27:1-5 explains that Brazen Altar was 5 cubits (7 ½ feet, long) the same length wide and 3 cubits (4 ½ feet, high). The altar was made of acacia or shittim wood, and was overlaid with bronze. Also horns were placed on each corner of the altar. The altar was place between the entrance gate and the Tabernacle. A common Israelite would enter the outer gate to the Brazen Altar where he was met by the priest. There he gave his sacrificial offering as a forgiveness of his sin.

The Brazen Laver, situated next to the Brazen Altar, was made of bronze mirrors and filled with water. This was used by the priests to wash their hands and feet before going in or coming out of the Holy Place according to Exodus 30:17-21.

Finally you have the Tent, or the Tabernacle structure, which was placed in the western part of the Tabernacle. The structure stood 30 cubits, 45 feet, in length and 10 cubits, 15 feet, in height and breadth. According to Exodus 26:36-37 The door was made of blue scarlet and purple thread, along with fine woven linen and stood upon 5 pillars which was made of acacia wood with gold hooks and bronze sockets. Only the priests were allowed to pass this through this door and enter the Holy Place to minister.

The Tent consisted of 2 parts; The Holy Place and the Most Holy Place. These 2 parts were divided by a curtain or veil, which Exodus 26:31-34 described as being made from blue, purple and scarlet linen with the cherubim artfully woven into the veil. This veil was symbolic of separating God from Man and was also known as "the curtain of Testimony."

Within the Holy Place was the Table of Shewbread, the Menorah, and the Altar of Incense. The Table of Shewbread was also known as the Table of Presence. As stated in Exodus 25:23-30, the Table of Shewbread was 2 cubits (3 feet) long, 1 cubit (1 ½ feet) wide and 1 ½ cubits (2 ¼ feet) high. It was made with acacia wood and overlaid with gold, along with a ring at each leg and poles made of acacia wood to carry the table. The purpose of the Table of Shewbread as explained in Leviticus 24:5-9, was for 12 pieces of showbread which represented the 12 tribes. They were made each week and were allowed to be eaten by the priests as it was a part of the Lord's offering.

The Menorah, or golden lampstand, was one piece of pure gold made into three (3) parts according to Exodus 25:31-40; the base, the central shaft, and the six branches. The menorah burned continually and twice a day the priest would tend to the wick and replenish it with olive oil.

The Altar of Incense was 2 cubits (3 feet) tall and 1 cubit (1 ½ feet) square. As stated in Exodus 30:1-10, the Altar of Incense was made of acacia wood, a crown around the top and 4 horns all overlaid with pure gold. Similar to the other pieces of holy furniture, the Altar of Incense had 4 rings laid with gold as well as 2 wooden sticks laid with gold to carry the furniture. The horns represented the 4 tribes (Judah, Reuben, Ephraim, Dan) and all of God's people. This altar was placed in front of the veil that separated the Holy Place from the Most Holy Place. The purpose of the altar was to burn incense. According to Exodus 30:34-38 the incense was made of a mixture of rare spices, mixed with frankincense, blended with fine powder and beaten with salt. Twice a day the priests would offer the incense and sprinkle the blood of the sin offering on the horn. This was the offering of the person whose sins had been forgiven by blood and who then went on to express the fragrance of love and worship, which was most pleasing to God.

The Most Holy Place, the Holy of Holies, or the Sanctum Sanctorum was a 10 cubit x 10 cubits (15' x 15') room that housed the most sacred piece of furniture, the Ark of the Covenant. The Ark was made of acacia wood overlaid with gold inside and out, according to Exodus 25:10-22. Inside the Ark contained two (2) broken tablets of the Law, a golden pot of manna and a budded piece of Aaron's rod. Sitting on top of the Ark of the Covenant was the Mercy Seat. Exodus

25:17-22 explains how the Mercy Seat was made of pure gold. On each side of the Mercy Seat was the cherubim who faced each other with their faces looking down upon the seat. The Cherubim, which represent the righteousness of God, is explained in Ezekiel 1:414 as angelic being with the face of a man, an ox, an eagle and a lion. Above the Mercy Seat sat the glory of God, *"And there I will meet with you, and I will speak with you from above the mercy seat, from between the two cherubim which are on the ark of the Testimony, about everything which I will give you in commandment to the children of Israel."* – Exodus 25:22.

Only the High Priest was allowed in the Most Holy Place one time a year, which was the Day of Atonement, which is properly explained in Leviticus 16:16, *"So he shall make atonement for the Holy Place, because of the uncleanness of the children of Israel, and because of their transgressions, for all their sins; and so he shall do for the tabernacle of meeting which remains among them in the midst of their uncleanness."*

As we can now see, the Tabernacle is an important piece not just to Masonry, but biblical history.

What makes this structure and the pieces thereof so amazing is how they are symbolic to Christ:

- The Entrance Gate – *"Jesus said to him, "I am the way, the truth, and the life. No one comes to the Father except through Me."* – John 14:6
- The Brazen Altar – *"I am the good shepherd. The good shepherd lays down his life for the sheep."* – John 10:11
- The Brazen Laver – *"Jesus replied, "I assure you, no one can enter the Kingdom of God without being born of water and the Spirit."* – John 3:5
- The Door of the Tabernacle - *"I am the door; if anyone enters through Me, he will be saved, and will go in and out and find pasture."* – John 10:9
- The Table of Shewbread – *"And Jesus said to them, "I am the bread of life. He who comes to Me shall never hunger, and he who believes in Me shall never thirst."* – John 6:35
- Menorah – *"Then Jesus spoke to them again, saying, "I am the light of the world. He who follows Me shall not walk in darkness, but have the light of life."* – John 8:12
- The Altar of Incense - *"Therefore He is also able to save to the uttermost those who come to God through Him, since He always lives to make intercession for them."* – Hebrews 7:25
- The Veil – *"Therefore, brethren, having boldness to enter the Holiest by the blood of Jesus, by a new and living way which He

consecrated for us, through the veil, that is, His flesh, and having a High Priest over the house of God, let us draw near with a true heart in full assurance of faith, having our hearts sprinkled from an evil conscience and our bodies washed with pure water." – Hebrews 10:19-22

- The Ark of the Covenant – *"And the Word became flesh and dwelt among us, and we beheld His glory, the glory as of the only begotten of the Father, full of grace and truth."* – John 1:14

The Tabernacle teaches us how to worship. Worship requires sacrifice. We enter into the gate with sacrifice, as Psalm 100:4 states, "Enter into his gates with thanksgiving, and into his courts with praise: be thankful unto him, and bless his name." We must be clean before entering his presence as Isaiah 1:16 explains, "Wash and make yourselves clean. Take your evil deeds out of my sight; stop doing wrong." So the next time you enter into a chapter of Royal Arch Masons, and you hear that it is assembled in a place representing the Tabernacle, you are in a place of worship. How will you enter?

-Holiness to the Lord -

Chapter 10

The Temple and the Tabernacle

"And let them make me a sanctuary and I will dwell among them."
– Exodus 25:9

One of Masonry's biggest symbols is King Solomon's Temple. We have witnessed the inner workings of its erection, its completion and its destruction. . The Temple, defined by Webster as, "the building devoted to the worship of God," is you and what you are to do through your actions. King Solomon's Temple is important as it symbolically describes the person you are supposed to be, but how many know that there is another important piece within Masonry, the Tabernacle?

In the book of Exodus chapters 25-30, we learn how Moses was given strict instructions to build the tabernacle that God may dwell with his people. According to Webster's Dictionary, a Tabernacle is, "a portable, or movable sanctuary." While in the wilderness, whenever Moses and the children of Israel traveled, the tabernacle traveled with them. The 12 tribes were responsible for carrying pieces of the Tabernacle during the day and when it was fully erected, the four (4) principles tribes guarded the four (4) cardinal directions. At the east guarding the entrance gate was the tribe of Judah, the tribe of Ephraim guarded the West, the tribe of Reuben guarded the South and the tribe of Dan guarded the North. No matter where the children of Israel were in the wilderness, God was with them as explained in Exodus 40:38 *"For the cloud of the LORD was upon the tabernacle by day, and fire was on it by night, in the sight of all the house of Israel, throughout all their journeys."*

King David erected a Tabernacle of his own after retrieving it from the household of Obed-Edom. David learned of the many blessing the household received because of the ark. As stated in 2 Samuel 6:17, *"They brought the ark of the LORD and set it in its place inside the tent that David had pitched for it, and David sacrificed burnt offerings and fellowship offerings before the LORD."*

The idea of building a Temple came from David, who said to his prophet Nathan in 2 Samuel 7:2, "Look," David said, *"I am living in a beautiful cedar palace, but the Ark of God is out there in a tent!"* That night God came to Nathan said in 2 Samuel 7:6, *"I have never lived in a house, from the day I brought the Israelites out of Egypt until this very day. I have always moved from one place to another with a tent and a Tabernacle as my dwelling."* God promised his people a secure place that would be free from enemies and it would not be disturbed.

We later come to find that although David thought of building, it was his son Solomon who was anointed to build as stated in 1 Chronicles 22:6-10, *"Then he called for his son Solomon, and charged him to build a house for the LORD God of Israel. David said to Solomon, My son, I had intended to build a house to the name of the*

LORD my God. But the word of the LORD came to me, saying, You have shed much blood and have waged great wars; you shall not build a house to My name, because you have shed so much blood on the earth before Me. Behold, a son will be born to you, who shall be a man of rest; and I will give him rest from all his enemies on every side; for his name shall be Solomon, and I will give peace and quiet to Israel in his days. He shall build a house for My name, and he shall be My son and I will be his father; and I will establish the throne of his kingdom over Israel forever."

We are all familiar with what took place afterwards. As Most Excellent Masters we've witnessed the glory of the house of Lord only to see it destroyed in our journey of becoming Holy Royal Arch Masons. We have now found ourselves in a place representing the Tabernacle erected by our ancient brethren. The question I pose to my Companions is: Do you understand the difference between the Tabernacle and the Temple?

The Tabernacle, as previously defined, means portable or movable. It has been shown that there were two (2) Tabernacles before the building of the Temple. Now, after the destruction of the Temple, we find ourselves in a third Tabernacle.

While both the Temple and the Tabernacle are considered places of worship, the Tabernacle is temporary, while the Temple is more secure and permanent. While we use the tools we have been to fit our minds for that spiritual building, it can be said that we too represent the Tabernacle. Why? Because this body that we are in is temporary, but wherever we go, the G.A.O.T.U. dwells with us. It is also good to note that both places of worship were well guarded, and everyone was not meant to enter. The same goes for you. Who you allow into your space is very important, and you must guard yourself well. So as you go from place to place throughout your life, know that the G.A.O.T.U. will continue to rest and abide with you.

-Holiness to the Lord-

Chapter 11

Words of the Veil

When arriving to Jerusalem from Babylon, the three (3) weary sojourners endeavored to make their way to appear before the Grand Council. In doing so they had to walk through the veils, and in order to gain admission into each veil the sojourners needed to be in possession of the several items of the previous veil. One of those items were the words of the veils, which we will now endeavor to explain.

Within the First Veil we use the pass "I Am That I Am." This, as we know comes from Exodus 3:1-15, when the Lord appeared to Moses out of the midst of a burning bush and commanded him to go before the Pharaoh and tell him to let His people go. Moses then asked as stated in Exdous 3:13-15, *"And Moses said unto God, Behold, when I come unto the children of Israel, and shall say unto them, The God of your fathers hath sent me unto you; and they shall say to me, What is his name? what shall I say unto them? And God said unto Moses, I AM THAT I AM: and he said, Thus shalt thou say unto the children of Israel, I AM hath sent me unto you. And God said moreover unto Moses, Thus shalt thou say unto the children of Israel, The LORD God of your fathers, the God of Abraham, the God of Isaac, and the God of Jacob, hath sent me unto you: this is my name for ever, and this is my memorial unto all generations."*

Within the Second Veil we use the words of the Master of the First Veil, "Shem, Ham and Japheth." These 3 were the sons of Noah who, according to Genesis 6, found favor with God. Noah had his sons when he was 500 years old, and was told by God how the world be destroyed by flood due to the wickedness of man. He was commanded to build an ark that would occupy his family along with 2 of each animal and insect to regenerate the world.

Shem, Ham and Japheth were considered the "Generations of Noah," or the "Table of Nations" as explained in Genesis 10. Their descendants, known as the Semities, Hamites and Japhethites, were responsible for the expansion of humankind and their dispersion into many lands after the flood. Shem bore five (5) sons, Ham bore four (4) sons, and Japheth bore seven (7) sons. From these sons come a total of 70 names, which has been said corresponds to Genesis 46:27 when the Israelites went down to Egypt and Exodus 24:9 when the 70 elders of Israel went up Mt. Sinai to meet with God.

Moses, Aholiab, and Bezaleel, words needed to enter into the Third Veil given by the Master of the Second Veil. As explained in Exodus 3, Moses was chosen by God to lead his people of Egypt into the promised land. During that journey at the top of Mt. Sinai he received instructions of law, as well as how to build a tabernacle. Among those instructions was the building of the Ark of Covenant and those in charge of building it, Bezalel and Aholiab.

Bezaleel, whose name means "in the protection of God, was the son of Uri, who's the son of Hur and from the tribe of Judah. As stated in Exodus 31:3-5, God, *"...filled him with the Spirit of God, with wisdom, with understanding, with knowledge and with all kinds of skills— 4 to make artistic designs for work in gold, silver and bronze, 5 to cut and set stones, to work in wood, and to engage in all kinds of crafts."* He was considered the chief architect of tabernacle and his primary duty was building the Ark of the Covenant. He was also in charge of holy oils, incense and priestly garments.

Assisting Bezaleel in building the Ark of the Covenant was Aholiab. Aholiab was the son of Ahisamakh and comes from the tribe of Dan. According to Exodus 38:23, Aholiab was, *"an engraver, and a cunning workman, and an embroiderer in blue, and in purple, and in scarlet, and fine linen."* Because of his skill Aholiab worked under Bezaleel as the deputy architect of the Tabernacle.

Finally, within the Fourth Veil we use the words Joshua, Zerubbabel and Haggai given by the Master of the Third Veil. Joshua was called to be the first high priest following the period of Babylonian captivity. He served as high priest for approximately 25 years was among the leaders who inspired the momentum to build the second temple according to Ezra 5:2. Next is Zerubbabel, whose name means "seed of Babylon." He was the son of Shealtiel and who after the proclamation from Cyrus, King of Persia, led over 42,360 captives from Babylon to Jerusalem as stated in Ezra 2:64. Zerubbabel was appointed governor of the Persian Province by King Darius of Persia, after which he began to build the second Temple in 521 BC after dealing with opposition from various tribes.

Lastly, there's Haggai, whose name means "my holiday." Haggai was the prophet during the building of the second temple. He was the first of three prophets after the Babylonian captivity and was considered one of the twelve (12) Minor Prophets. It was through Haggai that we learn more of Zerubbabel. Within the Book of Haggai Zerubbabel is called a son, a servant and God's signet ring, which signified a place of honor and authority. It said that this triad of names made Zerubbabel very important as he was a depiction of the future Messiah, Jesus. As Zechariah 6:12-13 states, *"And say to him, 'Thus says the Lord of hosts, "Behold, the man whose name is the Branch: for he shall branch out from his place, and he shall build the temple of the Lord. It is he who shall build the temple of the Lord and shall bear royal honor, and shall sit and rule on his throne. And there shall be a priest on his throne, and the counsel of peace shall be between them both."*

-Holiness to the Lord-

Chapter 12

Your Latter is Greater

"Who of you is left who saw this house in its former glory? How does it look to you now? Does it not seem to you like nothing? Be strong, all you people of the land,' declares the Lord, 'and work. For I am with you. Do not fear! The glory of this present house will be greater than the glory of the former house,' says the Lord Almighty. 'And in this place I will grant peace,' declares the Lord Almighty."

– Haggai 2:3-9

Each and every Companion can take the time to look at where they are now, and reflect on what it took to reach their place of prominence, whether personally or on a Masonic level. The journey was not easy for any of us, as a matter of fact many of us have been at what we thought was the pinnacle of our lives only to hit rock bottom and rise again. I could not help but compare the rise and fall of our lives symbolically to the ceremonies of a Holy Royal Arch Mason, let me explain.

During the ceremonies of exaltation, we are introduced to Zedekiah the last King of Judah. We learn that he was 21 years old when he was made King by Nebuchadnezzar II and reigned for 11 years. What's important to know that three (3) of Zedekiah's predecessors were removed from the throne for doing evil in the sight of God. Zedekiah, however did not learn from his predecessors and also did evil in the sight of God according to 2 Kings 25. Not only did Zedekiah refuse to listen to his prophet Jeremiah, but he rebelled against the very person who placed him on the throne. This angered the Lord, which lead to the destruction of the city and Temple. Zedekiah, realizing his mistakes, tried to flee along with sons, but they were overtaken. Zedekiah, before having his eyes plucked out, watched the killing of his sons. He was then bound in chains of brass and carried to Babylon where he was imprisoned until his death.

Many of us at some point in our lives have played the role of Zedekiah. We reached a certain status in our lives, whether it was financially, or a job promotion, or even social status. And instead of listening to the wise counsel that God sets before us or even using those who came before us as examples of what to do and what not to do, we decide not to heed the warnings. We decide that we've become higher than others because of what we've obtained, and even rebel against those who instrumental in getting us to where we were.

Like Zedekiah, we don't think about how our actions affect those who around us. Zedekiah lost sight of God's purpose for him and thought only of his agenda. Like him there has been a time when we lost sight because we have been consumed with our own agendas, and what we wanted didn't fall in line with God's will. Ultimately we found ourselves in a place where everything we seemed to cherish was taken away from us and placed in a state of imprisonment, whether its financially, emotionally, mentally or spiritually.

On a Masonic level, we can remember certain "Zedekiahs" who sat in the East. Those who put their own agendas in front of the agenda of the craft. Those who thought they were more powerful than the craft itself, and refused to take wise counsel from the ones who have passed the chair and rebelled against the very ones who placed in them in the position in the first place. These "Zedekiahs" lost sight of what's most important, which is the betterment of the craft. As result their lodge, chapter, Temple, etc. is destroyed and goes from flourishing meetings and wealth of knowledge to multiple roundtables and barely making it through a ritualistic opening. The craft then becomes imprisoned mentally when there's no light to shed among its members; emotionally, physically and spiritually when you have the faithful few working to accomplish what takes an entire membership to handle; and of course financially when members refuse to participate.

How many of you remember being at this point in your lives? How many of you remember your organization begin at this point? But even in that place of lowliness you should rejoice because the same God who allowed the destruction is the same God who brought us back to salvation. Our journey back to salvation was not easy. The Principal Sojourner told us the journey would be long, tedious and dreary and our roads rough, rugged and dangerous. Yet when we think of where we came from and where we're going, we will "endeavor to overcome every hardship and brave every new danger," for the purpose of rebuilding ourselves and our Order.

We've had many rivers to cross, broken bridges to get over, we've even had to come up on the rough side of the mountain to reach the place of our former glory. We learned through our ceremonies that the rebuilding of the house of the Lord took place near the ruins of King Solomon's Temple. A pastor once said, "Sometimes God will take you back to the place that brought you pain to redefine it and give you victory." Amos 9:11 states, *"In that day I will restore David's fallen shelter-- I will repair its broken walls and restore its ruins-- and will rebuild it as it used to be."* Just like that David's fallen shelter, God can repair, restore and rebuild us from the same place where we fell and make us greater.

The passages of Scripture used in the beginning of this lecture references those saw King's Solomon's Temple before it fell. They remembered its splendor, its materials and its greatness. Those same people were upset when looking at the foundation of the new Temple seeing it would not be like before, but God encouraged them to work and not fear because the present would be better than the former. Many people who are still in your life now may remember who used to be and try to compare the new you with the old you. Some older member of the Order will look at how things are now and compare it to before. But the reason you rejoice is because you know are no longer who you used to be. The reason you rejoice is because you no longer have to worry roundtables and lack of information. In your present state and prayerfully in the present state of the Order, you've been given peace.

So do as the scripture in Haggai 2 says, be encouraged, do not fear and work. Many people may not be happy with the person God has rebuilt. But just like King Solomon's Temple, you know within yourself that from your rise to your fall the sight of God was lost and it took you being imprisoned before you regained that sight. But all of this was in God's divine plan, you may not have all your material possessions, or your titles, or your status; your lodge, or chapter may not have the number of members it once had, but you have peace within yourself, you have the power to overcome, and because of that…YOUR LATTER IS GREATER!!!

-Holiness to the Lord-

Chapter 13

Walking the Veils

When the three (3) weary sojourners reached Jerusalem, they had to endeavor their way to the presence of the Grand Council. In doing so they had to pass through the Veils that guarded the sanctuary. As we are already aware, each veil represents a tribe and is represented by a specific color. It has always been my thought that the veils symbolically represent your walk through Masonry as well as through life.

The first veil, which through its color blue, could represent Symbolic Masonry, or your foundation. Here is where you began your journey, where you came out of your ignorance and took the first steps in making the best and the most of yourself. It was here you learned that life is a constant scene of trials. Here you learned how to curb your behavior, stand straight, walk upright, and spread brotherly love to all.

Of course you could gain admission into this veil without knowing the words, which I also believe is symbolic to your walk. The story of Moses and the burning bush has already been impressed upon your minds, but what's important about this lesson is how God reveals himself. Coming out of ignorance into moral and intellectual light is where God reveals himself and within Symbolic Masonry it's revealed the importance of paying homage to himself, of depending on Him, and of keeping Him first which happens to be the first paramount duty.

Having been given the knowledge and understanding, you're able to pass to the second veil. This veil is represented by purple symbolizing royalty, but in this case I find to represent something else. This particular veil, in my opinion, represents Cryptic Masonry. Those who are Royal & Select Masters know what takes in this Order prepares you for what happens in HRAM. This also ties in to the story leading to the words of this veil. God prepared Noah for what was getting ready to happen and heeded Noah to follow His directions.

In your walk of life, God will prepare for you what's coming next in your life. Like Noah, you may not be told when the next step in your life will take place, but if you trust Him and follow His instructions He will not lead you wrong. As Jeremiah 29:11 states, "For I know the plans I have for you, declares the Lord, plans for welfare and not for evil, to give you a future and a hope."

Being prepared for what's coming ahead you now pass through the third veil. Represented by scarlet, which signifies zeal, there are two life lessons learned in this veil that stems from Capitular Masonry. The first is that of the rejected stone, which we learn later becomes the cornerstone. This lesson coincides with the lesson of the second veil because like the rejected stone, there are those who will reject you because they don't understand you, what you do or why you do it. But as stated before it's not meant for you understand as long as you follow His instructions. Eventually when His plans unfold that's when you become the cornerstone.

The second lesson comes from working in the quarries. An actual quarry, according to Webster's Dictionary, is "an excavation or pit, usually open to the air, from which building stone, slate, or the like, is obtained by cutting, blasting, etc." As one of God's chosen people, given the proper tools to perform His work, could you not consider this earth a quarry? Remember we're fitting our minds as living stones and our work is to spread the truth, God's truth, to those who are uninitiated, so that they too may be living stones. We must be mindful of the quality of our work, not the quantity as told to us in the parable of the owner of the vineyard. We are also reminded by the words of the veils, who worked in building the tabernacle God commanded.

After working in the quarries and showing suitable specimen of your work, you pass within the fourth veil or sanctuary. White, as taught within HRAM, symbolizes purity of a contrite, or remorseful, heart. In your walk of life I look at this color to symbolize wisdom. Ecclesiastes 12:5 speaks of the almond tree, whose color is white, flourishing a symbol of old age or wisdom. In this veil you present the signet of truth, which was presented to you within the Scottish Rite. I acquaint this veil to the Scottish Rite because of the wisdom needed to obtain the knowledge within this Order. Upon reaching this veil, I'm reminded of a song that says, "As I look back over my life and I think things over. I can truly say that I've been blessed, I've got a Testimony." Before you receive the final password that admits you into the ineffable presence of Him, you can use that wisdom to teach others and whisper wise counsel to those following your footsteps.

Walking the veils, to me, is a similar to climbing the winding stairs of the middle chamber. As you climb the stairs you are unaware of what's around the corner. Similarly you are unaware of what's behind each veil, but just as you continue to climb you also continue to walk, reminding yourself of Proverbs 3:5-6, *"Trust in the Lord with all thy heart and lean not unto thine own understanding. And in all thy ways acknowledge Him and He shall direct your path."*

-Holiness to the Lord-

Chapter 14

What does it Mean to Be Exalted

"For all those who exalt themselves will be humbled, and those who humble themselves will be exalted."

– Luke 14:11

Recently a question was asked by a Companion why in this degree are we exalted? As I never thought about the reason why we are exalted, it sparked my interest to dive deeper into the meaning of exaltation.

Before entering this journey of becoming Holy Royal Arch Masons, you first had to be raised to the sublime degree of Master Mason. According to Webster's Dictionary, to raise means, "to set upright by lifting or building." From your initiation as EA, you've been building that temple within your mind, preparing yourself for that day when your temple becomes a piece of that spiritual building not made by hands. In order to be raised, you had to "die," meaning who you used to be could be no more as you were rising to become a new man on the square of morality.

Now you begin your journey into York Rite Masonry, which is considered to be the path of righteousness. During this journey, you learned how to work in the quarries and exhibit suitable specimens of your work before receiving your wages. You also learned through Matthew 20, that it's not the quantity of your work, but the quality.

After learning the wisdom of presiding in the Chair, and being present at the completion and dedication of King Solomon's Temple, it was time to begin your journey to being exalted. To be exalted, according to Webster's Dictionary, means: "to raise in rank, power or character." The first lesson is being exalted is being humble. Webster's Dictionary defines humble as: "showing that you do not think of yourself as better than other people." Your ceremony commenced by being placed into the humbling position of being stooped, and hearing the aforementioned passage of scripture. While you are taught that the principles secrets of this degree should be given in a certain manner, it really should press upon your minds two (2) things: 1. Before entering this journey, you had to be humbled which reminded you to be humble because as Proverbs 18:12 states, "before honor is humility." 2. You entered under a living arch, or better yet you entered under a covering. This should have taught you that no matter what you were getting ready to endure, you were covered or protected.

Throughout the ceremonies of this degree you witnessed examples of being humble and being humbled. Moses was humble when God revealed himself to him. Zedekiah and his people were humbled by God for their wicked ways by either being killed or placed into captivity for 70 years. The three (3) weary sojourners were humble enough to assist in rebuilding the house of the Lord without hope of fee or reward. Their willingness to work lead them to find the

Keystone, the Jewels of the three (3) Grand Masters and most importantly the copy of the Ark of the Covenant. Because of their humility, those weary sojourners were exalted to the Masters of the Veils.

Now you are exalted as a Companion of the Holy Royal Arch. Through your humility, you and your character have been raised to the level of Companion. It is said that there is no title greater than a Brother, but as Proverbs 18:24 suggests: "A man that hath friends must first shew himself friendly, and there is a friend (Companion) that sticketh closer than a brother." What does it means to be exalted? Being exalted has two (2) meanings. The first, as previously described, is the raising of your character and of your rank. You have gone from ignorance to knowledge to wisdom and through Proverbs 15:33 which states: "Wisdom's instruction is to fear the LORD, and humility comes before honor." You have learned that to truly be of great character you must think of more than just yourself. You have learned through these symbolic ceremonies that the work of the Lord is not easy. It is sometimes rough, rugged and dangerous, but take joy in Romans 8:18 which states: *"For I reckon that the sufferings of this present time are not worthy to be compared with the glory which shall be revealed in us."*

According to Webster's Dictionary, exalted also means, "to elevate by praise or in estimation, to glorify." By raising the Royal Arch you've learned to glorify that Great and Sacred Name of God. We glorify him each time we give the sign of a Royal Arch Mason. We remember that this House is Holy and the Lord is Holy. Holy is defined as: "exalted or worthy of complete devotion as one perfect in goodness and righteousness."

"Therefore having been exalted to the right hand of God, and having received from the Father the promise of the Holy Spirit, He has poured forth this which you both see and hear," as Acts 2:33 states. Also, *"The LORD is exalted over all the nations, his glory above the heavens,"* as Psalm 113:4 states.

Finally as Companions, being Holy means, "devoted entirely to the deity or the work of the deity." Our job is to do God's work, from working in the quarries, to presiding over his children, to completing our task and even rebuilding what was destroyed. As long as we remain humble in everything we do and exalt him in the process, we ourselves will be exalted.

-Holiness to the Lord-

Chapter 15

When the Work is Complete

"There is no more occasion for level and plumb line. For trowel or gavel, for compass or squares. Our works are completed, the stone safely seated. And we shall be greeted as workmen rare."

From the moment you started your journey in Masonry you had 3 goals in mind; to learn, to subdue your passions, and to improve yourself in Masonry. In order to accomplish these goals you were given certain tools and lessons, as well as learning about the building of King Solomon's Temple.

The first part of your journey was being initiated as Entered Apprentice. Here you were given what was needed for you to come out of ignorance. You were given tools that taught you how to properly divide your time and break off the pieces of who you used to be. You learned how to maintain your behaviors within certain boundaries, how to establish your presence by the points of your entrance, and the value of brotherly love. Finally it was explained to you that these tasks could be accomplished through mental and inward strength and being careful of your words and actions.

Next you were passed to the degree of Fellowcraft. Here you passed from ignorance to knowledge where you learned the importance of judgment. The tools presented to you reminded you to be upright, and display good behavior for what you did in this life would be judged in the next life. You learned that in life you would face prosperity and adversity, as well as some of the beauties of King Solomon's Temple. Finally when you displayed strict fidelity to your duties, you were given wages that helped you grow, renewed your strength, and gave you great feelings happiness.

The sublime degree of Master Mason was your next feat. Your raising from a dead level was a symbol of the old you dying and the new you raising up. You were taught that the three (3) paramount duties; God, your neighbor and yourself. You learned to make the best and most of yourself, that the character of a true man was found inside of you, and to imitate the character of GMHA, who was all about integrity. Finally you were given the tool spread brotherly love and affection throughout the world to unite us into one common band.

Your journey, however, was not yet over as your temple was incomplete. So you went further and advanced to the degree of Mark Master Mason. Here you learned that the quality of your work was more important than quantity. You were presented with the chisel and mallet, which continued the work that the common gavel could not finish. King Solomon's Temple is nearly complete, and with the stone that the builders rejected, it now becomes the cornerstone for the Temple.

You now have witnessed the completion of the Temple when you were received and acknowledged as a Most Excellent Master. You remove your apron for you no longer have to wear the craftsmen clothes. The work that you have set out to do is complete and there is nothing left to do but receive your wage.

King Solomon's Temple has been used throughout Masonry to show that the true Temple is YOU! We have learned that Masonry is a way of life, and through life you have passed through different degrees. Being initiated, you came out of ignorance by making up your mind to change who you used to be. You redevelop your mind by changing your habits, actions and behaviors. After a level of maturity you passed to the degree of knowledge. You understand right from wrong, you realize that what you say and how you act is watched by others and will later be judged. You have the reached the point of raised, or being saved, or baptized. That's when the real work begins, the work of showing others the God inside you by your actions.

The work of exalting the G.A.O.T.U. so that he can draw all men unto him as stated in John 12:32. And it's not about how many people you influence, but the quality of people you influence. And when the work is complete, we yearn for the day we hear, *"Well done, good and faithful servant; thou hast been faithful over a few things, I will make thee ruler over many things: enter thou into the joy of thy lord."* in Matthew 25:23

So are you working? Are you doing good work, true work, square work? When others see you, are they reminded of Matthew

5:16? You have been given the tools, the lessons and the instructions to build your spiritual and mental temple. This work as well know is not easy, but when our labors are finished, it's time to lay down our tools and be judged, like The Williams Brothers said, "May the work I've done speak for me."

-Holiness to the Lord-

Chapter 16

Judah, Ephraim, Rueben and Dan

As Companions we are familiar with our chapter room representing the tabernacle. We are familiar with the veils and banners and how they are emblematically teach us of the 12 tribes who bore their banners in the wilderness, namely Judah, Ephraim, Rueben and Dan. Why out of the 12 tribes were these four chosen to be represented within HRAM?

It must first be understood that the 12 tribes of Israel were the descendants of Jacob. After Jacob stole the birthright and blessing from Esau he fled and during his flight he grew tired. He rested upon a stone and during his sleep he had a dream. This dream consisted of a ladder with angels ascending and descending. According to Genesis 28:13-15, *"At the top of the stairway stood the Lord, and he said, "I am the Lord, the God of your grandfather Abraham, and the God of your father, Isaac. The ground you are lying on belongs to you. I am giving it to you and your descendants. Your descendants will be as numerous as the dust of the earth! They will spread out in all directions—to the west and the east, to the north and the south. And all the families of the earth will be blessed through you and your descendants. What's more, I am with you, and I will protect you wherever you go. One day I will bring you back to this land. I will not leave you until I have finished giving you everything I have promised you."* When he woke he realized that place was a gateway to heaven, and according to Genesis 28:18-19, he took that stone, poured olive oil over it as a memorial and named that place Bethel, meaning the "house of God."

Jacob, whose name was changed to Israel because as Genesis 33:28 states, *"he struggled with God and with humans and have overcome,"* was the father of twelve sons. Their names were Reuben, Simeon, Levi, Judah, Issachar, Zebulun, Joseph, Benjamin, Dan, Nephtali, Gad and Asher. These represented the 12 tribes in Israel with the exception of Joseph. Genesis 48:5-6 explains how Jacob adopts Joseph's sons Ephraim and Manasseh, which divided Joseph's tribe into half. It explains why the name of this tribe is interchangeable and is sometimes known as the "House of the Joseph."

Let us now look into the first tribe, Judah. Judah, whose name in Hebrew means "thanksgiving" or "praise," was the fourth son of Jacob and his first wife Leah. In Genesis 49 Jacob calls his sons to him to bless them. In verses 8-10, Jacob blesses Judah by saying, *"Judah, your brothers shall praise you; Your hand shall be on the neck of your enemies; Your father's sons shall bow down to you. Judah is a lion's whelp; From the prey, my son, you have gone up. He couches, he lies down as a lion, And as a lion, who dares rouse him up?"* Hence the reason the symbol of the tribe of Judah is the lion with the crown and scepter representing the King of Kings as Psalm 60:7 proclaims, *"...and Judah, my scepter, will produce my kings."*.

From the tribe of Judah came the prophets Isaiah, Amos, Habakkuk, Joel, Micah, Obadiah, Zechariah, and Zephaniah. Most importantly from the tribe came David and his royal line known as the "House of David," and Jesus affectionately known as the "Lion of Judah."

During their time in the wilderness, the tribe of Judah guarded the East side of the tabernacle, which was the only entrance into the tabernacle. This is where Moses, Aaron and his sons, and the priests were stationed. The standard-bearer for the tribe was Nahshon, the son of Amminadab according to Number 2:3. Guarding the entrance to the tabernacle along with the tribe of Judah were the tribes of Issachar and Zebulun.

Guarding the South side of the tabernacle was the tribe of Reuben. Reuben, whose name means, "behold, a son," was Jacob's first born son. He was responsible for saving his brother Joseph's life when the rest of his brothers wanted to put him to death due to their jealousy. However, his father Jacob because of his act of incest with his father's concubine Bilhah, the mother of Dan and Nephtali, did not bless Reuben. Genesis 49:4 explains, "Turbulent as the waters, you will no longer excel, for you went up onto your father's bed, onto my couch and defiled it."

Elizur was the standard-bearer for the tribe of Reuben, whose symbol was the man for as Genesis 49:3 states, *"Reuben, you are my firstborn, my might, the first sign of my strength, excelling in honor, excelling in power."* Along with the tribe of Reuben, the tribes of Simeon and Gad guarded the south side of tabernacle as Number 2:12-14 explains.

At the West side of the tabernacle was the tribe of Ephraim. Ephraim, whose name means "Fruitful," was the youngest son of Joseph. As stated earlier in the lecture their grandfather Jacob adopted him and his older brother Manasseh, and although Ephraim was the youngest, Jacob elevated Ephraim as Genesis 48:19-20 states, *"However, his younger brother shall be greater than he, and his descendants shall become a multitude of nations. He blessed them that day, saying, "By you Israel will pronounce blessing, saying, 'May God make you like Ephraim and Manasseh!'" Thus he put Ephraim before Manasseh."* This blessing makes the tribe of Ephraim important next to Judah, causing David to say in Psalm 60:7, *"Ephraim, my helmet, will produce my warriors."* One well known Ephraimite is Joshua, who was given the lead of the people of Israel by Moses and victorious in the battle of Jericho.

Elishama, son of Ammihud, was the standard-bearer for the tribe of Ephraim, whose symbol was the ox, symbolizing patient industry and strength. The tribes of Manasseh and Benjamin also guarded the West side of the tabernacle as explained in Number 2:20-22

Finally we have the tribe of Dan who guarded the North side of the Tabernacle. Dan, whose name means "God is my judge," was the fifth son of Jacob and his mother, as mentioned earlier, was Bilhah, Rachel's maid and Jacob's concubine. Jacob's blessing to Dan is explained in Genesis 49:16-17, *"Dan shall judge his people, as one of the tribes of Israel. Dan shall be a serpent by the way, an adder in the path that biteth the horse heels, so that his rider shall fall backward."* Samson, a Danite, was one of the most famous judges in Israel.

The tribe of Dan had several symbols. In the passage of scripture previously stated, their symbol was a serpent, or adder. In Deuteronomy 33:22, their symbol was a lion's whelp. In the wilderness and on their, which was bore by Ahiezer the son of Ammishaddai, their symbol was the eagle symbolizing swiftness and wisdom. The tribes of Asher and Neptali guarded with the tribe of Dan according to Number 2:27-29.

Judah, Reuben, Ephraim, and Dan. Out of the twelve (12) tribes, these four were considered very important, not just because of the positions in which they guarded the tabernacle, but take a look at their symbols. The lion, the man, the ox and the eagle, as seen in the vision of Ezekiel as the cherubim as explained in Ezekiel 1:10, *"Their faces looked like this: Each of the four had the face of a human being, and on the right side each had the face of a lion, and on the left the face of an ox; each also had the face of an eagle."* The Cherubim were the guardians of God. They are seen in Genesis guarding the Garden of Eden after the banishment of Adam and Eve. They are seen surrounding God's throne in Ezekiel's vision. So it would only be natural that since the Ark of Covenant was considered God's dwelling place, there would you find His guardians, in the form of the four chosen tribes, protecting Him.

-Holiness to the Lord-

About the Author

Damien Jack is a Past Excellent High Priest of Excelsior Chapter No. 44 in Charlotte, NC. He has been a Holy Royal Arch Mason since January 9, 2010 and currently serves as the Excellent Grand Lecturer for the Most Excellent Grand Chapter of Holy Royal Arch Masons of North Carolina, PHA. PEHP Jack is also an honorary member of the Most Excellent Grand Chapter of Holy Royal Arch Masons of South Carolina. PEHP Jack's achievements include Excellent High Priest of the Year (2015), Past Excellent High of the Year (2015) and under his leadership, Chapter of the Year (2015)

Made in the USA
Coppell, TX
17 July 2021